Nuns Having Fun

By Maureen Kelly and
Jeffrey Stone

WORKMAN PUBLISHING • NEW YORK

*To my angels—Ethan, Hannah, and Abigail—*M.K.

*To Anne Stone—*J.S.

Library of Congress Cataloging-in-Publication Data
Kelly, Maureen, 1957-
   Nuns having fun / by Maureen Kelly and Jeffrey Stone.
      p. cm.
   ISBN 978-0-7611-5041-1 (alk. paper)
 1. Nuns--Humor. I. Stone, Jeff, 1955- II. Title.
   PN6231.N94K45 2008
   255' .900207--dc22

                                          2007050348

Workman books are available at special discounts when purchased in
bulk for premiums and sales promotions as well as for fund-raising or
educational use. Special editions or book excerpts also can be created
to specification. For details, contact the Special Sales Director at the
address below or send an e-mail to specialsales@workman.com.

Workman Publishing Company, Inc.
225 Varick Street
New York, NY 10014-4381
workman.com

Printed in U.S.A.

First printing May 2008

10 9 8 7 6

⁂ Chapter and Verse

················ ❖ ················

Introduction

"Fun" is not a concept generally associated with nuns. For those who remember the habited Sisters of yore from their Catholic school days, strict, scary, and secretive are more like the words that come to mind. There was always an otherworldly mystique about nuns, a way of life set apart from everyone else. Nuns were members of an exclusive club with elaborate codes, clothing, and initiation rites. Who could not be fascinated?

Our first experience of nuns was as the stern mentors of our youth in parochial school and CCD classes. As adults, we reminisced about our experiences with these formidable women of the cloth in a humor book called *Growing Up Catholic*. We always knew there was a lighthearted side to convent life, which is celebrated here in these vintage photographs of nuns at play and at leisure. There is something about Sisters caught in the act of cutting loose and letting their hair down, so to speak, that appeals to the whimsy, nostalgia, and retro sensibility of Catholics and non-Catholics alike.

Here are nuns from a bygone era, reveling in unexpected moments of delight and relaxation—a snowball fight, road tripping, frolicking in the surf, motorcycle riding, poker playing, even target shooting. We've also included "Chapter and Verse" of nun lore and trivia, along with features like "Wimple Watch," "Take My Order, Please," and "Women Who Could Have Been Nuns."

Although few nuns today wear the traditional habit, the iconic black-and-white robed figure is everywhere in pop culture—from movies and TV to greeting cards, Sister Mary Margarita cocktail napkins, and the boxing nun puppet. The reality is that hundreds of thousands of Catholic nuns continue to dedicate their lives to the service of God and others, especially those most in need around the world.

So sit up straight and pay attention, whether you are a former bold-as-brass parochial school hellion or have never met a woman in a wimple. Let's exult, indulge, and give thanks for these fun-loving nuns in all their high-spirited splendor.

—Maureen Kelly and Jeffrey Stone

"I brake for Catholics."

Hook, line, and Sisters

"O Lord,
keep me on
the straight
and narrow."

Ale Marys

"So what if the
waves aren't parting,
Sister Martha!"

Convent Confidential

Crossing herself
at every turn

Every volley
shall be exalted.

Going downhill fast

Sisters of
Perpetual Indulgence

There's no business
like God's business.

"O Lord,
won't you buy me
a Mercedes-Benz?"

"Sisters Are Doin' It for Themselves"

Many are called,
but few are frozen.

Nuns on the rocks,
with a splash

Know Your Nuns
A Field Guide

THE SPORTY NUN

With her square jaw, muscular build, and no-nonsense demeanor, Sister Robert Anne means business, whether she's on cafeteria duty, reigning over the chemistry lab, or coaching the field hockey team in her black Converse high-tops. A genuine sports nut, she not only knows what a Hail Mary pass is, but can actually throw one. Stern but good-natured, she holds pizza parties for her kids when Notre Dame wins a big game.

THE DEVOUT NUN

She may not be a martyr in the literal sense of the word, but Sister has a lot to offer up. She prays for her unruly young charges with a vengeance, and faithfully attends every pious devotion, from Novenas to Nocturnal Adoration. In Sister's class, rehearsal for the crowning of Mary in the May procession eclipses preparation for the yearly standardized tests, much to parents' dismay. Along with memorizing the state capitals, Sister's students compete to learn the patron saint for every conceivable malady. Winners are awarded scapulars, holy cards, and vials of holy water from Lourdes, which they dribble on each other's foreheads to "cure" cases of typhoid, malaria, and smallpox.

THE STICKLER

Whether it's a uniform skirt that's a millimeter too short or a test paper without the requisite "JMJ" at the top, she seems to delight in finding fault in the smallest things. Her world is exclusively black-and-white, like her habit. She lines the chalk pieces up from smallest to largest and insists on a tidy cloak room. With her antibacterial gel pump always at the ready, you'll never catch her with a used Kleenex up her sleeve. Don't be tardy!

THE INGENUE

Increasingly rare, the young nun is a welcome breeze through the musty parochial school corridors. Hip and with-it, she knows who the Foo Fighters are and has seen *High School Musical* (1 and 2). The middle school girls adore her, and pour out their hearts to her at recess. Versed in the latest teaching methods, she demanded a smart board for her social studies class. She chaperones the annual class trip to Washington, D.C., but with a side trip to Hershey, Pennsylvania. Pray that she stays.

THE SCHOLAR

A brilliant Latin teacher with a Ph.D. from Georgetown,

Sister could be heading up the State Department, but instead coaches the debate team and dreams of grooming a future Supreme Court justice. Her gold wire-rimmed glasses and studious air belie a super-competitive edge, and she's never more delighted than when her team absolutely obliterates the competition's logic. Her team's motto: *veni, vidi, vici.*

THE THEATRICAL NUN

She's directed all the school musicals for the past twenty years, and regularly rebuffs bribes from parents who want their daughters to be cast as Maria in *The Sound of Music.* Dramatic on stage and off, she uses different voices, and gestures with her hands a lot. Floaty, colorful scarves lend flair to her somber habit. Back in the day, she performed in *Hair* on Broadway. Even now, she has been known to frequent piano bars.

THE MISSIONARY

Returning from her mission in Africa to teach at a suburban parochial school for a year, she marvels at the indoor plumbing and reminds her pupils that there are more important things in life than choosing the right color for your iPod. She wears Birkenstocks and a colorful *dashiki,* a word she makes the kids learn how to spell.

Everything You Always Wanted to Know About Nuns
but Were Afraid to Ask

Do you have hair?

Is it hot under your habit?

What do you wear to bed?

How do you go swimming?

Do you get to choose where you live?

When do you "know" you are going to be a nun?

What do you carry in your pockets?

Who does your laundry?

Why are you called a bride of Christ?

What do you confess in Confession?

Are pets allowed in the convent?

How many outfits do you have?

Do nuns retire?

By the NUN-BERS

Nuns worldwide in 1975: 968,526
Nuns worldwide in 2000: 801,185

Nuns in the U.S. in 1965: 179,954
Nuns in the U.S. in 2007: 63,699

Teaching nuns in the U.S. in 1965: 104,000
Teaching nuns in the U.S. in 2002: 8,200

Catholics per nun in the U.S. in 1965: 239
Catholics per nun in the U.S. in 2000: 761

Estimated number of women in 2000 in initial
formation (taking the first steps toward
becoming a nun) in the U.S.: 2,700

Number of years it takes to become a Sister in
a typical religious community: 3 to 9

Median age of active religious women in 1999: 69
Average age of the Dominican Sisters of Saint
Cecilia (a traditional Dominican order) in 2007: 36

Increase in number of Dominican
Sisters of Saint Cecilia since 1992: 79%

Numbers of times per day
Benedictine Sisters pray together: 3

The year that Mother Angelica, a conservative nun
who achieved national fame on the Eternal Word
Television Network (EWTN), changed her order's
habit to a more traditional style: 1993

Cost of one Our Lady of Guadalupe Seed
Pendant Necklace, sold by the National
Coalition for Church Vocations: $3

Amount of money per day that a nun impostor
in a religious habit can make panhandling
in the New York City subway: $600

Number of Consecrated Virgins* in the Catholic
Church in the U.S. in 2007: 150+
Number of Consecrated Virgins* in the Catholic
Church in the world in 2007: 3,000+

*These women are not nuns and are totally self-supporting, but have
pledged their virginity to God in order to dedicate themselves to the
service of the Church. Some people think they have the worst of both
worlds—a life of celibacy and a mortgage to boot.

Sources, see page 256

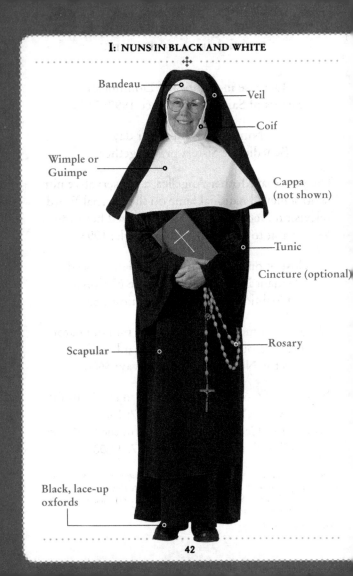

I: NUNS IN BLACK AND WHITE

Bandeau

Veil

Coif

Wimple or Guimpe

Cappa (not shown)

Tunic

Cincture (optional)

Scapular

Rosary

Black, lace-up oxfords

Making a Habit of It
The Parts of a Nun's Wardrobe

❖

BANDEAU: The stiff band of fabric that stretches over the forehead, frequently fastened beneath the veil at the ears.

VEIL: Long cloth that covers the head and trails down the back.

COIF: Cap beneath the veil, which hugs the head and is often tied under the chin.

WIMPLE OR GUIMPE: The bib-like piece that extends over the neck and chest, and occasionally covers the chin.

TUNIC: The basic building block of the nun's wardrobe, this dresslike garment covers Sister from shoulder to toe.

CINCTURE: Belt made of leather, cloth, or rope tied around the waist of the tunic.

SCAPULAR:* From the Latin for "shoulder," this long, smocklike garment is layered over the tunic in both front and back.

CAPPA: Latin for "cape," an outer cloak or mantle worn over the tunic.

ROSARY: Prayer beads ranging in size from modest to massive, often attached to the cincture.

BLACK, LACE-UP OXFORDS: Not officially part of the habit, but *de rigueur* for nuns everywhere.

---

*The lay version of the scapular features two small cloth squares worn around the neck as a holy devotion.

Judi Dench

Ruth Bader Ginsburg

Janet Reno

Women Who Could Have Been Nuns

Marcia Cross

Glenn Close

Christiane Amanpour

America Ferrera

Condoleezza Rice

Maggie Gyllenhaal

Whether it's a combination of strictness and sweetness or something a little otherworldly, there's an indefinable quality that makes for a good nun—and these women have it.

Cynthia Nixon

Ann Curry

Jennifer Hudson

Taking her cue
from on high

Sisters on the
dock of the bay

"He maketh me
to dance in
green pastures."

"Okay, who
forgot the
Saint Christopher
statue?"

What happens in Vegas,
stays in Vegas.

Pure as the
new-fallen snow . . .
but with a wicked slider!

"Look, Mother Superior,
no praying hands."

Bar nun

Lead us not
into temptation.

"Everybody Was
Nun Fu Fighting"

Cleanliness
is next
to godliness.

God's on *our* side.

"All together,
Y-M-C-A!"

"For God's sake,
get me to the church
on time!"

"Sister Michael,
row that boat ashore."

Wimple Watch
How to Tell an Order by Habit

DAUGHTERS OF CHARITY OF ST. VINCENT DE PAUL

Paper airplanes, anyone? Or origami, perhaps? This headdress was the basis for the name "Flying Nun."

GREY NUNS OF MONTREAL

Though these nuns are every bit as sanctified as any other Sister, some folks may see a hint of the vampire in the black headdress.

LITTLE SISTERS OF THE POOR

The dramatic black cape inspires the nun with superhero tendencies.

SISTERS OF BON SECOURS

The dramatic fluted cap tied under the chin, paired with natty white cuffs, identifies these Sisters as a fashion-forward French order.

MARYKNOLL SISTERS

Crowned by their prowlike headdresses, these Sisters forge ahead in their missionary work.

SISTERS OF CHARITY

For the nun who prefers a simple black cap to the whole veil thing.

SISTERS OF CHARITY OF THE BLESSED VIRGIN MARY

The stiff, square, boxlike headdress gives the illusion that Sister is always on television.

SISTERS OF CHRISTIAN CHARITY

The fanciful white bow tie lends a debonair accent to this otherwise no-nonsense habit.

POOR HANDMAIDS OF JESUS CHRIST

The veil fastens under the chin, framing the face in a Little Red Riding Hood sort of way.

DOMINICAN SISTERS

Pure, simple, and timeless. The religious equivalent of the little black dress and a string of beads.

Is She or Isn't She?
How to Tell a Nun Out of Habit

◆◆◆

These days, it's less common to see a Sister in traditional habit. Still, there are those who claim they can always pick out a nun, even in street clothes. Just look for these telltale traits:

Short, no-nonsense hairdo

Longish skirts

Low-heeled shoes

Clear nail polish

Minimal makeup

Penchant for dark-colored pantsuits

Excellent posture

Wears simple gold or silver "wedding" band

Cross or religious emblem pinned to her lapel

Smells of Ivory soap and talcum powder

Perfect penmanship

Blushes at off-color jokes

Travels in packs

Loves labyrinths, dream-catchers, and mystics

Convent Makeovers

A Sister wants to look good as well as do good. But no face and figure are perfect (except in the eyes of God), so here's a bit of divine guidance to help solve some of the most common challenges faced by style-conscious nuns everywhere.

PROBLEM: Too short
SOLUTION: The diminutive nun need not be troubled by her tiny stature, which surely belies an indomitable spirit. A towering headdress will add precious inches to her compact frame. (*Warning:* Headdress may cause swaying, especially on blustery days.)

PROBLEM: Stout, no waist
SOLUTION: A cinctured black habit neatly creates the illusion of an hourglass figure for the nun cursed with an ill-defined waist. Bold rosary beads further accentuate the waistline, whether created by God or Sister herself.

PROBLEM: Droopy jowls
SOLUTION: Wear a headdress that sweeps upward, lifting any sagging features. The winged wedge made famous by *The Flying Nun* will take years off any visage.

PROBLEM: **Too tall**
SOLUTION: The heavenly altitude of the 6-foot-plus nun can be brought down to earth by a headdress that closely skims the top of the head and sits low on the forehead. A shortish, full veil will draw attention to the face and a bold red cincture will break up the height lines. Black oxfords with quarter-inch heels can be special ordered and are worth the extra expense.

PROBLEM: **Multiple chins**
SOLUTION: The middle-aged nun troubled by the first hints of aging should seek out a wimple that rises up to the chin, elongating the neck and firming the jaw line. This Ace-bandage–type wimple will disguise even a triple chin.

PROBLEM: **Small face, delicate features**
SOLUTION: The dainty nun should opt for a soft, prairie-style bonnet or ruffled cap. An extra-large cross will help distinguish her from the Amish or an extra on *Little House on the Prairie*.

Take My Order, Please
Inspired Names of *Real* Religious Communities

◆◆◆

Cistercian Nuns of the Strict Observance, O.C.S.O.

Daughters of Divine Zeal, F.D.Z.

Handmaids of the Precious Blood, H.P.B.

Benedictine Nuns of the Primitive Observance, O.S.B

Mothers of the Helpless, M.D.

Oblates of the Mother of Orphans, O.M.O.

Sisters of the Guardian Angel, S.A.C.

Sisters of Mary Immaculate, M.I.C.M.

Dominican Sisters of the Perpetual Rosary, O.P.

Sisters of the Lamb of God, A.D.

I Should Have Ordered That
Alternative Orders
for the Irreligious

◆◆◆

Sisters of Perpetual Indulgence

Order of the Ecstatic Aesthetics

Sisters of the Sick and Tired of Being Poor

Sob Sisters of the Bleeding Heart

Perplexed Sisters of the Sorrowful Mysteries

St. Clare's Order of the Deplorable

Wielders of the Terrible Swift Ruler

Ecumenical Sisters of Shalom

Faithful Servants of the Fervent Observance
(of Television)

What's in a Nun's Name?

Euphemia. Clothilde. Cunegunde. Where did nuns ever get names like that? In the old days before Vatican II, a nun was required to take a new name to symbolize the start of her life of poverty, chastity, and obedience—not to mention occasional skeet-shooting, snowshoeing, and shuffleboarding. Some nuns got to pick their own saint's name, while others had their names chosen for them by their superiors.

The list of Marys, in homage to the Blessed Virgin, was endless. But there could only be so many Mary Catherines, Mary Roses, and Mary Margarets. Hence Wilhelmina and Prostasia.

Some nuns even had men's names, with gender-bending monikers like Mary Patrick, Thomas Marie, and Robert Anne. That's because each Sister took the name of a saint she was expected to emulate, and it didn't matter whether the saint was male or female. Isn't it fascinating that nuns, living in a pre-feminist world with strict male and female roles, felt free to take men's names centuries before

Whitney, Taylor, and Sydney became popular names for girls?

These days, most Sisters keep their birth names. But as laudable as that practice may be, it also means that in the future we're unlikely to meet nuns with such colorful and memorable names as these:

"They Don't Make Nun Names (Like That No More)"*

Sister Eustochium
Sister Macrima
Sister Donata
Sister Philomena
Sister Hildegard
Sister Euphrasia
Sister Eucharia
Sister Radegund
Sister Ancilla
Sister Walburga
Sister Blandina
Sister Stanislas
Sister Ildephonsus
Sister Thaddeus

Sister Muir
Sister De Moffit
Sister Trinita
Sister Cornelius of the Reparatrix
Sister Alphonsus
Sister Alta Maria
Sister Aquinata
Sister Rose of Lima
Sister John of the Cross
Sister Mercedes
Sister Marionette

* with a nod to the 1977 hit song by Tommy Sharp

"It looks like
Sister Robert Anne
by a veil."

Sister Mary Peter, Sister Mary Paul, and Sister Mary Mary

"*Nunsense* is my favorite show!"

A hook and
a prayer will give
Sister a spare.

"Come on, Sister,
do the locomotion!"

Knit nun, purl two.

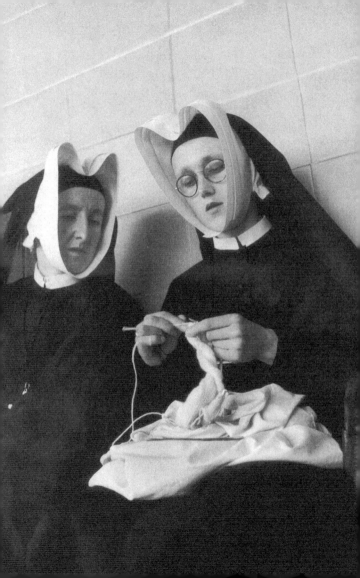

"Just think of it as
a little vacation
within a vocation."

"And He will
raise me up."

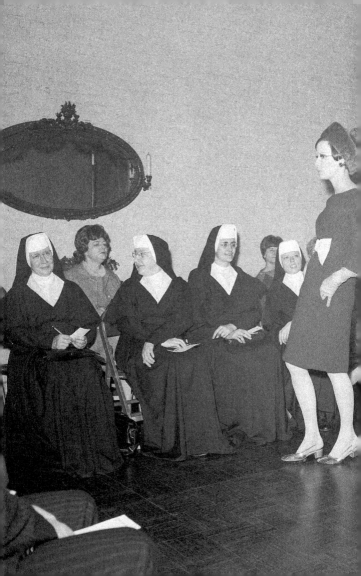

"Drop the hem,
add a veil,
and it's perfect."

Holy Smokes!

MTV Nunplugged

"Be sure
to leave room for
the Holy Spirit."

Twister Sisters

On a slippery slope

"Three more coins
for the collection box!"

"Am I my
Sister's goalkeeper?"

Missing Questions from the Baltimore Catechism

237. Who made Sister?

God made Sister.

238. Why did God make Sister?

God made Sister to save the souls of Catholic schoolchildren and make sure they have perfect Palmer Method penmanship.

239. What is Sister's greatest time-saver?

Sister's greatest time-saver is that she does not have to decide what to wear every morning.

240. Why is Sister an excellent driver?

Sister is an excellent driver because of her superb peripheral vision, honed by years of darting sharp glances around the classroom.

241. Why has Sister never gotten a speeding ticket?

Sister has never gotten a speeding ticket because no self-respecting police officer would ever give her one.

242. Why is it good to sit next to Sister on a turbulent airplane flight?

It is good to sit next to Sister on a turbulent plane flight because Sister will help you make a perfect Act of Contrition as the oxygen masks drop.

243. Why does Sister appear to glide rather than walk?

Sister appears to glide rather than walk in order to appear serene, and so that her rosary beads don't clank and give away her location.

244. What is Sister's least favorite chore in the convent?

Sister's least favorite chore in the convent is getting the grass stains out of the scapulars after the Sisters' annual Dominicans vs. Franciscans softball game.

245. What does Sister do in her spare time?

In her spare time, Sister founds hospitals and schools, ministers to the sick and poor, fights injustice, promotes nuclear disarmament, and works to bring about world peace.

246. What does Sister think of nun humor?

Sister says, "To err is human, to laugh is divine."

"Offer it up."

TRANSLATION: In Catholic theology, suffering—from acne to heartache—can earn you points in the afterlife.

Nun-sense?
What Sister Says—What She Means
PART I

"Always bring a dime and a phone book on a date."

TRANSLATION: The phone book goes between you and the boy if you sit on his lap. The dime stays between your knees at all times. If it drops, use it to call home immediately.

"Your body is a temple . . . of the Holy Spirit, that is."

TRANSLATION: Don't even *think* of going to second base.

"Leave room for the Holy Ghost."

TRANSLATION: There should be at least a foot of air between you and your date when dancing.

"Keep your legs crossed."

TRANSLATION: So you won't have to use the rhythm method of birth control.

⁜

You Did What?
Sister's Favorite
Classroom Punishments

———◆◆◆———

Getting swatted with ruler

Gum on nose

Writing out 100 "Hail Marys" on blackboard

Mowing convent lawn

Dusting church pews

Confiscation of *Cosmo Girl*

Contents of personal notes read out loud to class

Not allowed to attend Vocation Day

Eraser in mouth

FOR VENIAL SIN:
Standing in corner in wastebasket

FOR SINS OF A MORE GRIEVOUS NATURE:
Standing with nose in a circle on the chalkboard

"Jesus is watching you."

TRANSLATION: And He doesn't like what He sees.

Nun-sense?
What Sister Says—What She Means
PART II

"I have eyes in the back of my head."

TRANSLATION: Just try throwing a spitball, and not even your Guardian Angel can protect you from my wrath. What else explains my supernatural ability to detect silent shenanigans in the classroom with my back turned?

"Eat your lunch."

TRANSLATION: It may be a squashed peanut butter sandwich, but you should regard it as a gift from God because there are starving children in the world.

"Examine your conscience."

TRANSLATION: Count all the ways you have wronged me— I mean, the Lord.

"Bold as brass."

TRANSLATION: You're one venial sin away from permanent detention.

Vocational Vocabulary
Increase Your Religious Word Power

Religious life has a language all its own, and some of the terms can be mystifying. Test your knowledge of church terminology and see how you stack up spiritually.

1. ABBESS
a. A large pimple or boil
b. Female head of a monastery

2. ABSOLUTION
a. A nun's black-and-white philosophy of life
b. Forgiveness of sin

3. ASCETIC
a. Fancy vinegar from Italy
b. One who lives a life of extreme poverty and simplicity

4. BEATIFICATION
a. What happens at the day spa
b. Last step to becoming a saint

5. CALCED
a. Certain orders of nuns who wear shoes
b. Supplement for osteoporosis

6. CANONIZE
a. To formally recognize as a saint
b. To blast to kingdom come

7. CARMELITE
a. An order of nuns
b. Sticky, low-calorie candy

8. CONTEMPLATIVE
a. Having a bad attitude
b. One who is devoted to prayer and reflection

❖

9. CONVENTUAL
a. Adhering to standard sensibilities of the day
b. Of or relating to a convent

10. DISPENSATION
a. An exemption from Church law
b. The process of ejecting a Pez

11. DOWRY
a. What a young woman brings to the convent
b. What a young woman doesn't want to look like in the convent

12. EREMITIC
a. Hermit-like
b. Pleasantly scented

13. EXORCISE
a. Jogging or tennis, for example
b. Drive out the devil

14. HAGIOGRAPHY
a. Biography of a saint
b. Memoirs of a shrew

15. MENDICANT
a. Someone who lies
b. Member of a religious order who lives by begging

16. MODIFIED HABIT
a. Religious garb adopted in the 1960s
b. Limiting yourself to one pack a day

17. MONASTIC
a. Nun or monk who lives in a monastery
b. Boringly repetitive

18. POSTULANT
a. A person taking the first steps to become a nun
b. Standing up straight

SCORE CARD

0–5 correct: Heathen

5–9: Back-pew Catholic

10–14: Just a little more time in Purgatory

15 or more: Sister's pet

Answers: 1b, 2b, 3b, 4b, 5a, 6a, 7a, 8b, 9b, 10a, 11a, 12a, 13b, 14a, 15b, 16a, 17a, 18a

"You are my cross to bear."

TRANSLATION: She's you-know-who, you're Pontius Pilate.

Nun-sense?
What Sister Says—What She Means
PART III

"Whoever buys the most pagan babies wins!"

TRANSLATION: Pagan babies were non-Catholic children from Third World countries who were "bought" and baptized thanks to Catholic schoolchildren's money. Often part of a competition.

"This is the happiest day of your life."

TRANSLATION: What Sister tells you on the day you make your First Holy Communion.

"You're puting another nail in the Cross."

TRANSLATION: You're tormenting our Savior every time you talk back to Sister.

"Jesus, Mary, and Joseph!"

TRANSLATION: The names of the Holy Family, sure, but also one of the few acceptable Catholic profanities.

"Bless me, Father
for I have
sinnnnnned."

Mass transit

"Personal foul, Sister!
That'll be ten Hail Marys."

On a swing
and a prayer

"Protect us, O Lord,
for we are upright women—
at least for now."

The original Flying Nuns

White women
can't jump.

Talk about a
Hail Mary pass!

Shall we gather
at the Riverdance?

A pride of nuns
goeth before the fall.

Blow, Sister Gabriel, blow!

"We are family.
I got all my
Sisters and me."

No backsliding.

"Sister Marina,
give us back
our beach towels!"

"Yes, Juanita,
I think you
would enjoy life
in the convent."

Favorite Nuns of the Silver Screen

M any of our most popular actresses have eagerly sought roles as Sisters, whether flying through the air, making play clothes out of draperies, or hiding out from the mob. Who could forget these immortal performances?

Sally Field
as Sister Bertrille
in *The Flying Nun*

Ingrid Bergman
as Sister Mary Benedict
in *The Bells of St. Mary's*

Julie Andrews
as Sister Maria
in *The Sound of
Music*

Whoopi Goldberg
as Sister Deloris
in *Sister Act*

Deborah Kerr
as Sister Clodagh
in *Black Narcissus*

Ellen DeGeneres
as Sister Louise
in *Will and Grace*

Audrey Hepburn
as Sister Luke
in *The Nun's Story*

Robbie Coltrane
as Sister Euphemia
in *Nuns on the Run*

Susan Sarandon
as Sister Helen
Prejean in *Dead
Man Walking*

Debbie Reynolds
as Sister Luc-Gabrielle
in *The Singing Nun*

They Wanted to be Nuns

These celebrated women once considered entering the convent or, in Catholic terms, they "got the calling." But their fans are glad that they answered the call from Hollywood instead.

"When I was really little, I wanted to be a nun. But then my sister told me that nuns didn't get paid, and so I said, 'Forget that!' I wanted to be a businesswoman."

Eva Mendes

"How could I have been anything else but what I am, having been named Madonna? I would either have ended up a nun or this."

Madonna

"I have been to the Vatican a few times and I have gotta say, I saw some nuns there and I wanted to run up to them and say, 'Take me!'"

Anne Hathaway

"I still love anything connected to nuns. That's why I love all of Yohji Yamamoto's designs—they look like a nun's habit, and if I had my way, I'd always dress like a nun."

Catherine Keener

"When I was a young girl of twelve or thirteen I wanted very much to be a Catholic priest. Of course this was impossible, so I wanted to be a nun."

Anne Rice

⁜

Speaking of Sisters . . .

"I saw nuns as superstars. When I was growing up I went to a Catholic school, and the nuns, to me, were these superhuman, beautiful, fantastic people."
Madonna, *singer*

⁜

"I don't have a life, I really don't. I'm as close to a nun as you can be without the little hat."
Gabrielle Reece,
professional volleyball player

⁜

"The sixties were when hallucinogenic drugs were really, really big. And I don't think it's a coincidence that we had the type of shows we had then, like *The Flying Nun.*"
Ellen DeGeneres, *comedian*

✥

"None of us got where we are solely by pulling ourselves up by our bootstraps. We got here because somebody—a parent, a teacher, or a few nuns—bent down and helped us pick up our boots."

Thurgood Marshall, *former Supreme Court Justice*

✥

"Nuns and married women are equally unhappy, if in different ways."

Christina of Sweden,
17th-century queen

✥

"Hearing nuns' confessions is like being stoned to death with popcorn."

Fulton J. Sheen,
Former Archbishop of Rochester, NY

Above and Beyond the Calling

Sisters Who Were Saints

ST. ELIZABETH ANN SETON
Raised an Episcopalian, she managed to "have it all" by marrying and raising five children before being widowed, founding the Sisters of Charity, and becoming the first American-born saint.

ST. CLARE OF ASSISI
Known for the clarity of her visions, she is the patron saint of eye diseases, needle workers, and television writers. Foundress of the Poor Clares, she reminded her Sisters not to overdo the self-denial "for our bodies are not made of brass."

ST. TERESA OF AVILA
No slave to fashion, she founded the Discalced (barefoot) Carmelites and made all her nuns give up shoes.

ST. THERESE OF LISIEUX (THE LITTLE FLOWER)
She died young, but her famous autobiography showed that sainthood is attainable by anybody. Maybe you?

ST. RITA OF CASCIA
Before finding serenity in the convent, Rita had a life worthy of a soap opera: forced by her parents to marry against her will, she endured an abusive marriage, the assassination of her husband, and the death of her twin sons. Talk about a desperate housewife!

ST. CATHERINE OF SIENA

She suffered from the invisible stigmata—feeling the pain of Jesus' wounds with no visible signs—and became the patron saint for people with bodily ills.

ST. MARGARET MARY
Reportedly somewhat humorless, she was considered by some of her Sisters to be delusional. But who's laughing now?

ST. GERTRUDE THE GREAT
Although she was brought to the convent at the age of five and apparently never left, she ironically became the patron saint of travelers.

ST. FRANCES CABRINI
An immigrant from Italy, she was the first citizen of the United States to be canonized a saint. *Brava, Soire Francesca!*

Holy Rollers

Twisted Sister

For thine
is the kingdom
and the powder
and the glory.

"Ready, aim, fire
and brimstone!"

"Will holy oil work?"

Biker Chicks

"I will lift up
mine eyes
unto the hills."

Nun-o-meter

Defender of the Faith

D-O-G is my copilot.

"Hit me with
your best shot!"

" . . . five, six, seven
 . . . go to heaven."

"No, they can't see up your habit, Sister Helga!"

"Now that's
what I call waltzing,
Sister Matilda."

"This is
even more fun
than walking
on water."

The Swinging Nun

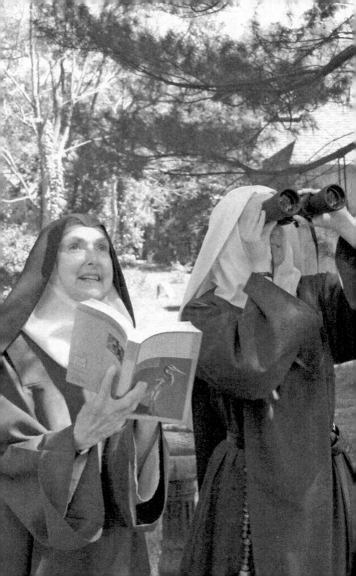

"Wait!
Is that a dove or
the Holy Spirit?"

Playing it close
to the vestments

Vocations on Vacation

When they want to catch a little R & R, nuns have their habitual haunts, just like everyone else. Here are some of their favorites.

THERE'S NO PLACE LIKE ROME

No need to book a hotel—just stay in your order's motherhouse in Rome. First stop: The Vatican! In St. Peter's Basilica, try not to be jealous that the Swiss Guard uniforms are so much prettier than yours. Just this once, hold back three coins from the collection box to throw in the Trevi Fountain, and wish for the first female pope. Come nightfall, if the Spirit moves you, hike up your habit for a quick plunge.

A BITE OF THE BIG APPLE

One of the great shopping meccas, NYC holds a special allure for Sisters, due to its array of world-class religious articles stores. Start with early Mass at St. Patrick's Cathedral to fortify you for a whirlwind tour of shops featuring a cornucopia of statues, relics, and rosaries. Thank heavens it's only a venial sin to max out the convent credit card.

DIVINE DECADENCE

In preparation for Ash Wednesday's penitence, partake of a little Mardi Gras indulgence in New Orleans. It's okay to grab for the gold and purple beads at the parade, but do not—repeat, do not—remove your wimple, no matter how many people yell, "Take it off, Sister!"

SAILING HOLY WATERS

Having taken a vow of poverty does not preclude the gift of a cruise from a well-heeled parishioner. The pious Sister might soak up the history of the early martyrs in Mediterranean port cities, whereas the burnt-out teacher might prefer a cruise to the Bahamas, where she can enjoy drinks on deck curled up with the latest (Vatican-banned) Dan Brown novel.

DISNEY WORLD WITHOUT END

Who says Sister can't play in the Magic Kingdom while praying for the Heavenly Kingdom? You'll want to make the Sign of the Cross before entering the Haunted Mansion, and say a perfect Act of Contrition before careening down Space Mountain. Be sure to wear your habit—you'll get whisked to the front of every line, no *FAST-PASS* needed! Plus, you'll get as many requests for pictures as Mickey does.

Things Sister Would Secretly Love to Do

Have more than one glass of wine at dinner

Sleep in on a Sunday morning

Curse freely when another driver cuts her off

Not make her bed

Stay in a hotel room by herself

Sing tunes from *Hairspray* at Vespers

Get a tattoo of praying hands on her ankle

Take a ride on a Harley

Put up a Facebook profile

Go trick-or-treating in her habit

Try on a pair of Jimmy Choo's

Sister's Wish List

Vows of poverty notwithstanding, Sister is mortal, after all, and not immune from worldly desires.

GPS system to locate Catholic churches anywhere in the world

Karaoke machine for learning tricky *Messiah* parts

Black Crocs for gardening

EWTN cable TV subscription

iPod for downloading Vatican podcasts

Built-in air conditioner for her habit, like Disney's cooled Mickey Mouse costume

Subscription to *This Old Habit* magazine

Aromatherapy kit to scent the convent with the fragrances of incense, burnt palms, and beeswax

Sister's Sudoku

Though a fan of numerical Sudoku, Sister prefers to use religious symbols, as in this game.

Directions: Simply complete the grid so that each column, each row, and each 3-by-3 grid contains one of each of the nine symbols.

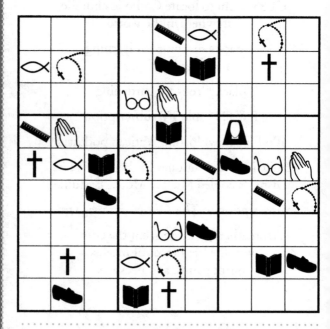

Sister's Word Search

Idle hands are the devil's playthings, says Sister.

Directions: Busy yourself by searching for these words, which can be found horizontally or vertically in the grid.

CONVENT	ROSARY BEADS	MASS
HABIT	RULER	SIGN OF THE CROSS
CRUCIFIX	PRAYERS	VATICAN II

```
D B E V V T A F L O T L W E Z
A V T A U F G H U J K E M N O
R C C T B U H L I P R U L E R
M R E I P F A G S T O N M Y U
A U T C O M B R P E S L B O H
Y C R A I D I T Q U A J C E V
S I G N O F T H E C R O S S P
I F K I R F G R I B Y M O K D
B I S I V L E M O P B A C R N
T X O S A D C O N V E N T Y E
E B I W E L O Y J S A R D U S
C R E D Y F M H I V D S A V O
A M C B P R A Y E R S Y U H M
N C E I H F S T A J E V R A C
U B V A R K S H I R L N A E W
```

Did You Hear the One About . . . ?

COMPLAINTS, COMPLAINTS

A young nun enters a convent where she can only utter two words every ten years. After the first decade, she visits Mother Superior and says, "Bed hard."

Ten years later, she says, "Food bad."

After 30 years, she goes to the Mother Superior and says, "I quit."

"I'm not surprised," says Mother Superior. "You've been complaining ever since you got here."

SPEED DEMONS

A cop pulls over a carload of nuns. "Sister, this is a 55 mph highway. Why are you going so slow?"

The Sister replies, "Sir, I saw a lot of signs that said 41, not 55."

The cop answers, "Oh, Sister, that's not the speed limit, that's the name of the highway you are on!"

The Sister says, "Oh! Silly me! Thanks for letting me know. I'll be more careful."

At this point, the cop looks in the backseat where the other nuns are shaking and trembling and asks, "What's wrong with your friends back there? They're shaking something terrible."

Sister answers, "Oh, we just got off Highway 101."

HOLY COW!

The wise old Mother Superior was dying. The nuns gathered around her bed, trying to make her comfortable. They gave her some warm milk to drink, but she refused it.

Then one nun took the glass back to the kitchen. Remembering a bottle of whiskey received as a gift, she opened it and poured a generous amount into the warm milk. Back at Mother Superior's bed, she held the glass to her lips. Mother drank a little, then a little more, and before they knew it, it was all gone. "Mother, Mother," the nuns cried, "give us some wisdom before you die!"

She raised herself up in bed with a pious look on her face and, pointing out the window, she said, "Don't sell that cow."

MIRACLE CURE

While Pat is waiting in the doctor's reception room, a nun comes out of the doctor's office. She looks very ashen, drawn, and haggard.

Pat goes into the doctor's office and says to the doctor, "I just saw a nun leaving who looked liked she'd seen the Holy Ghost or something. I have never seen a woman look worse."

The doctor says, "I just told her that she is pregnant."

Pat exclaims, "Oh my, is she?"

The doctor replies, "No, but it sure cured her hiccups."

What do you give a nun on Valentine's Day?

A dozen rosaries

What do you call a nun who walks in her sleep?

A roamin' Catholic

What do you call a nun with a frock made of titanium?

A hard habit to break

What do you call a nun at a costume party?

A blessing in disguise

What do you call a nun with a sprained ankle at a rock concert?

Twisted Sister

What do you call towns inhabited by nuns?

Sister cities

What do you call a nun who just passed her bar exam?

A Sister-in-law

Kicking back
with a little Blue Nun

"Okay, who brought
the loaves?"

View from the pew

"Heigh ho,
heigh ho,
it's off to church
we go."

"The Wind Beneath My Veil"

Heaven's Angels

"Ain't got a
blessed thing
if it ain't got
that swing."

Shred it, Sister!

"Heavens!
A sacrifice fly!"

"Who says nuns
can't hold their liquor?"

Leap of Faith

"American Idol,
here I come!"

"After Vespers,
the Council will decide
who gets kicked off
the island."

And she shall rein
for ever and ever.

"I sure wish
we hadn't given up
mittens for Lent."

Guided by GPS
(God Positioning System)

Still kickin' it

"Whither thou mowest,
I will mow."

And God said,
"Thou shalt not wear
Speedos after thirty."

"Yo, we'll have three loaves and fishes, and some pretzels, too."

About the Authors

Maureen Kelly and Jeffrey Stone are coauthors of the *New York Times* bestseller *Growing Up Catholic* and the *Nuns Having Fun* calendars.

Maureen was baptized at Most Precious Blood Church in Denver. Her first confession was said at St. Pius X Church in Dallas, and she received her First Holy Communion at Holy Ghost Church in Houston. In parochial school, she won a glow-in-the-dark plastic Madonna for selling Holy Childhood Christmas Seals and was a member of the Junior Altar Rosary Society, an organization of young Catholic girls dedicated to straightening church pews and dusting kneelers. She went on to graduate from St. Agnes Academy. She has worked for several book publishers and is now a freelance writer and editor living in Pittsburgh.

Jeff was born in Rhode Island and grew up in Maine. He was baptized at Sacred Heart Church in East Providence, despite the fact that the priest contended that neither Jeffrey nor Allen (his middle name) was a saint's name. Among Catholic school students, Jeff was known as a "public"—a public school student who attended religious education (CCD) classes at a Catholic school on Saturday—and was frequently accused of messing up the parochial kids' desks. He has worked in book publishing for many years and is currently a freelance writer and editor living in New York City.

Sources for "By the NUN-BERS," page 41: Statistics from the Center for Applied Research in the Apostolate (CARA) at Georgetown University, the *2007 Catholic Almanac, Leading Catholic Indicators: The Church Since Vatican II* by Kenneth C. Jones, *The Habit* by Elizabeth Kuhns, and various websites including www.culturalcatholic.com.

Credits

Front Cover: Jock McDonald Film, Inc.
Back Cover: Gerd Pfeiffer/Voller Ernst
Spine: Gerd Pfeiffer/Voller Ernst
Title Page: Ian Murphy/Getty Images

Photography:
AKG Images 168 right, 169 top left; Olycom 37 bottom, 69, 183; AP/Wide World Photos 10, 36, 44 bottom center, 44 bottom left, 44 top center, 44 top left, 44 top right, 45 bottom center, 45 bottom left, 45 top right, 63, 91, 109, 121, 125, 129, 143, 154, 164 left, 164 right, 165 center, 165 right, 179, 217, 231, 241, 243, 247; Black Star, J. Bruce Baumann/Stockphoto.com 151; Buffalo & Erie County Historical Society 173; Corbis 7, 9, 15, 19, 26, 29, 32, 38 bottom, 48, 57, 74, 93, 101, 102, 105, 132, 141, 145, 147, 148, 163 bottom, 164–165, 168 bottom, 171, 177, 184, 207; Ron Sachs/CNP 45 top center; Jenna Bascom 245; Pat Doyle 251; Paul Kaye/Cordaiy Photo Library Ltd. 97; Mark Savage 45 bottom right; Koren Ziv/Sygma 44 bottom right; Getty Images 95, 113, 195, 201, 221, 227; Scott Gries 45 top left; Ian Murphy 22; Imagestate, Rachel Morton/Impact Photos 5, 192; IPNStock, Melissa Farlow/Aurora 21; Jock McDonald Film Inc. 199; Juli Eirich 31, 61, 234; Jupiter Images 42; Library of Congress 222; Lili Almog 110, 138, 202, 228, 249; Linda Vukaj 35, 189; Magnum Photos, Burt Glinn 53; Mirror Pix 232, 237; John Dempse 106, 191; NBC Photobank, Chris Haston 162 center; Omni-Photo Communications, Tom Stillo 174; Peter Arnold Inc., A. Riedmiller 205; Photofest, ABC 160; Gramercy Pictures 163 top left; RKO Pictures Inc. 161 top right; Twentieth Century Fox Film Corp 161 top left; Warner Bros. 162 bottom; Redux Pictures, Jack Manning/The New York Times 65; Retna Ltd, Camera Press 16, 25, 47, 66, 117, 137, 153, 159, 219, 238; Cruzeiro 70; Reuters, Max Rossi 206; Rex USA, John Dee 73; Julian Makey 135; David McEnery 98; Frank Monaco 88; Liz Reynolds 187; Shutterstock.com 37 top, 83, 208; Sister Barbara Joseph Foley, CST 180; The Carnegie Library of Pittsburgh 58, 131; The Image Works, Ospedale di D. Maria della Scala/Alinari 169 center; Mary Evans Picture Library 68 left; K-B. Karwasz/SV-Bilderdienst 253; Topham 87, 169 bottom right; Voller Ernst, Claudia Tadini de Raota 197; Gerd Pfeiffer 13, 51, 214; Keystone Pressedienst 54.

Illustrations:
pp. 80–81, 123: Wesley Bedrosian
pp. 76–78, 210: Eric Brown